CHINA
WORLD ADVENTURES
BY STEFFI CAVELL-CLARKE

BookLife

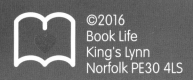

©2016
Book Life
King's Lynn
Norfolk PE30 4LS

ISBN: 978-1-78637-007-5

Written by:
Steffi Cavell-Clarke

Designed by:
Drūe Rintoul

A catalogue record for this book
is available from the British Library.

CHINA
WORLD ADVENTURES

CONTENTS

Page 4   Where is China?

Page 6   Weather and Landscape

Page 8   Clothing

Page 10   Religion

Page 12   Food

Page 14   At School

Page 16   At Home

Page 18   Families

Page 20   Sport

Page 22   Fun Facts

Page 24   Glossary and Index

Words in **bold** can be found in the glossary on page 24.

WHERE IS CHINA?

China is a one of the largest countries in the world. China is between India, Mongolia and Japan.

MONGOLIA

JAPAN

CHINA

BEIJING

The capital city of China is Beijing.

The **population** of China is more than one billion. China has the highest population in the world.

WEATHER AND LANDSCAPE

Mount Everest is the highest mountain in the world.

China is very large so it has lots of different landscapes. It has rivers, mountains, deserts and forests.

Each of these landscapes has a different **climate**. The mountains are very cold and the deserts are very hot.

HALLELUJAH MOUNTAINS

THE GOBI DESERT

CLOTHING

Many people who live in China wear comfortable and practical clothing. Sometimes, traditional clothing is worn on special occasions.

There are many different types of traditional clothing in China, but mostly, the clothes are made out of silk covered with **embroidery**.

In China, the colour red is believed to ward off evil spirits.

CHEONGSAM

RELIGION

China is home to many religions. The religions with the most followers are Confucianism, Taoism and Buddhism. But everyone in China celebrates Chinese New Year.

Chinese New Year lasts for fifteen days and involves lots of celebrations. Families come together to watch street parades and firework displays.

Dragon dances are performed to scare away evil spirits.

FOOD

A Chinese meal often has a few small bowls of rice, noodles and some vegetables. A popular dish in China is a stir-fry.

Chinese food is traditionally eaten with chopsticks. Chopsticks are long thin wooden sticks. They are held in one hand and used to pick up small pieces of food.

CHOPSTICKS

AT SCHOOL

Children in China start school at the age of six. They study Chinese, English, geography, maths and art.

Every Monday morning, children at primary school raise the Chinese flag and sing the **national anthem**.

The Chinese flag is red with five yellow stars.

AT HOME

In the cities, many Chinese people live in flats. There are so many people in China that sometimes more than one family has to share one flat.

In the small villages, houses are often made out of wood and stone. They have a tiled roof and a small garden called a courtyard.

FAMILIES

In China, Grandparents are treated with respect and kindness. They are often cared for by other members of the family at home.

Families like to get together to celebrate special occasions. They celebrate by eating special food and playing games together.

SPORT

Chinese martial arts are a traditional sport in China. Martial arts is a fighting technique, which can be used to protect yourself.

Chinese martial arts are also called kung fu.

Children in China like to fly kites after school. Chinese kites are bright and colourful.

KITE FLYING IN CHINA

FUN FACTS

The Great Wall of China was built thousands of years ago. The Great Wall is 13,170 miles long.

It is so long that it can be seen from space.

China is home to the Giant Panda, the only place where it still lives in the wild.

Pandas love to eat bamboo.

GLOSSARY

climate: the weather in a large area

embroidery: a raised pattern sewn into fabric

national anthem: a song that represents a country

population: amount of people living in that place

traditional: ways of behaving that have been done for a long time

INDEX

Chinese flag: 15

Chinese New Year: 10, 11, 19

chopsticks: 13

families: 11, 16, 18, 19

food: 12, 13

Mount Everest: 6

The Great Wall of China: 22

Photocredits: Abbreviations: l-left, r-right, b-bottom, t-top, c-centre, m-middle.
All images are courtesy of Shutterstock.com.

Front Cover, 24 – Jay Venkat. 1 – Aleksey Klints. 2 – Nila Newsom. 3, 8 – Ami Parikh. 5 – Radiokafka. 6, 10 – saiko3p. 7t – Dchauy. 7b – Lena Serditova. 9 – stockyimages. 11 – wong yu liang. 12br – Dinesh Picholiya. 12tr, 12bl – HLPhoto. 13 – szefei. 13inset – Simone van den Berg. 14 – steve estvanik. 15t – Ailisa. 15b – Lena Serditova. 16 – Kunal Mehta. 17 – NOWAK LUKASZ. 18 – Monkey Business Images. 19 – Dragon Images. 19inset – Rehan Qureshi. 20 – Rosli Othman. 21 – Maksym Gorpenyuk. 21inset – Kostsov. 22 – KAMONRAT. 23 – Raphael Christinat.